THE
HOUND DOG'S
HAIKU

and

Other Poems

for Dog Lovers

paw prints on the stairs
each fainter . . . like years: dogs are
dreams to which we wake

in tribute to all the dogs I've been lucky
to know at Hopewell Springs
M. J. R.

To the dogs who have shared my life, all too briefly . . .
Spicy, Spot (yes, Spot), Little Dog Mollie, Ralph, Selkie, Hilda, and Fred
M. A.

Text copyright © 2011 by Michael J. Rosen
Illustrations copyright © 2011 by Mary Azarian

First edition 2011

Library of Congress Cataloging-in-Publication Data is available.

Library of Congress Catalog Number 2008940378

ISBN 978-0-7636-4499-4

11 12 13 14 15 16 CCP 10 9 8 7 6 5 4 3 2 1

Printed in Shenzhen, Guangdong, China

This book was typeset in ITC Esprit.
The illustrations are woodcuts printed in black, then colored with acrylic paint.

Candlewick Press
99 Dover Street
Somerville, Massachusetts 02144

visit us at www.candlewick.com

THE HOUND DOG'S HAIKU

and Other Poems for Dog Lovers

MICHAEL J. ROSEN

illustrated by MARY AZARIAN

CANDLEWICK PRESS

Table of Contents

PARSON RUSSELL TERRIER

ENGLISH SPRINGER SPANIEL

WEIMARANER

SAMOYED

SHIH TZU

DALMATIAN

MINIATURE SCHNAUZER

DACHSHUND

fresh hay fills your house
nose and paws feather the nest
circling fields in dreams

BLUETICK
COONHOUND

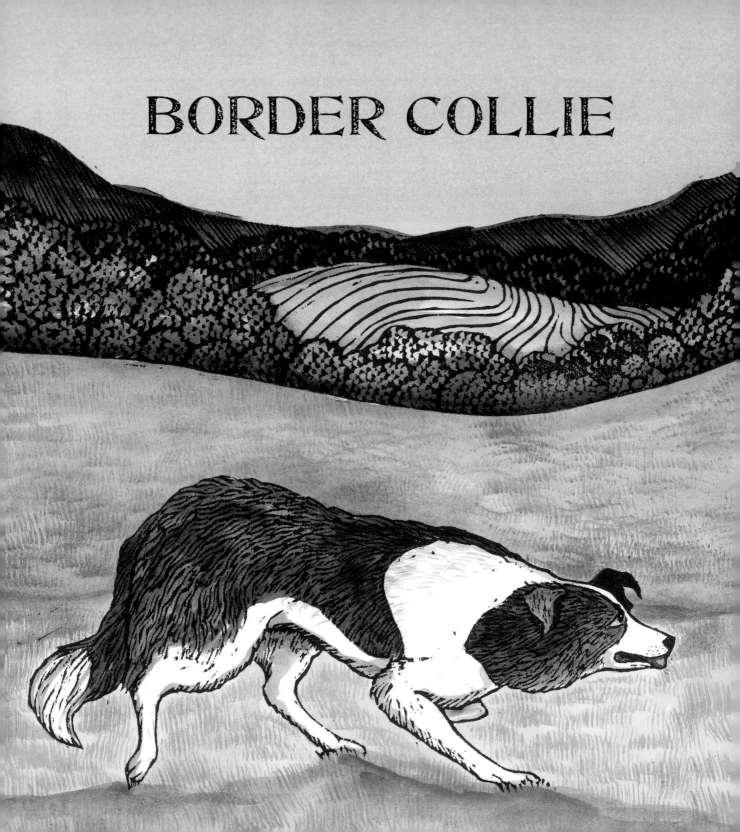

BORDER COLLIE

above your fixed gaze
a Milky Way of cows move—
your constellations

SIBERIAN HUSKY

January find
young deer's antler in the snow
grinning dog's forked tongue

GREAT PYRENEES

the first duck splash-lands
speck in the iced pond's lone eye
soon . . . the chase restarts

BEAGLE

far off, one dog barks
dreams blur like smoke from chimneys
he barks at barking

OLD ENGLISH SHEEPDOG

dog day *before* noon:
cool sun warming your *left* side
dog day *after*noon . . .

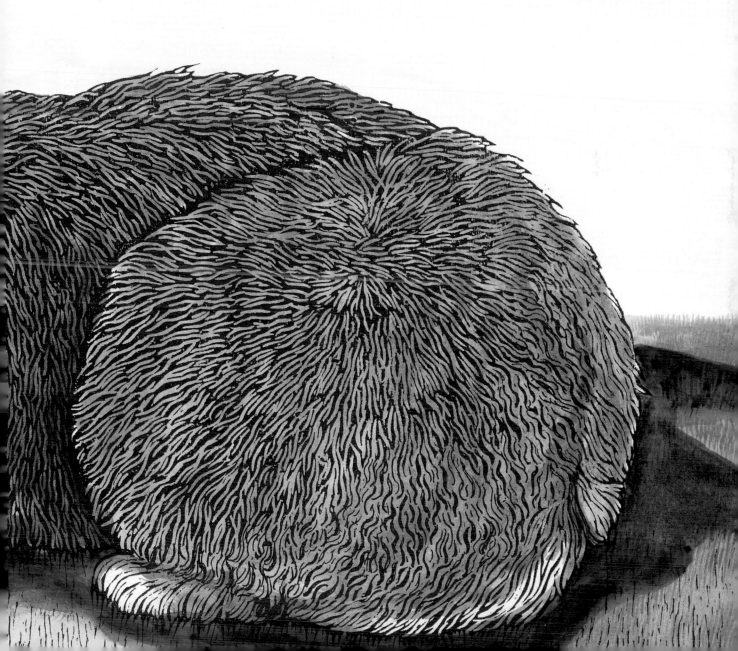

milk-sweet puppy breath
needle-sharp teeth and toenails:
neither lasts for long

STANDARD POODLE

dozing, paws outstretched,
you soar across cloud-pillows
superhero dreams

PEMBROKE WELSH CORGI

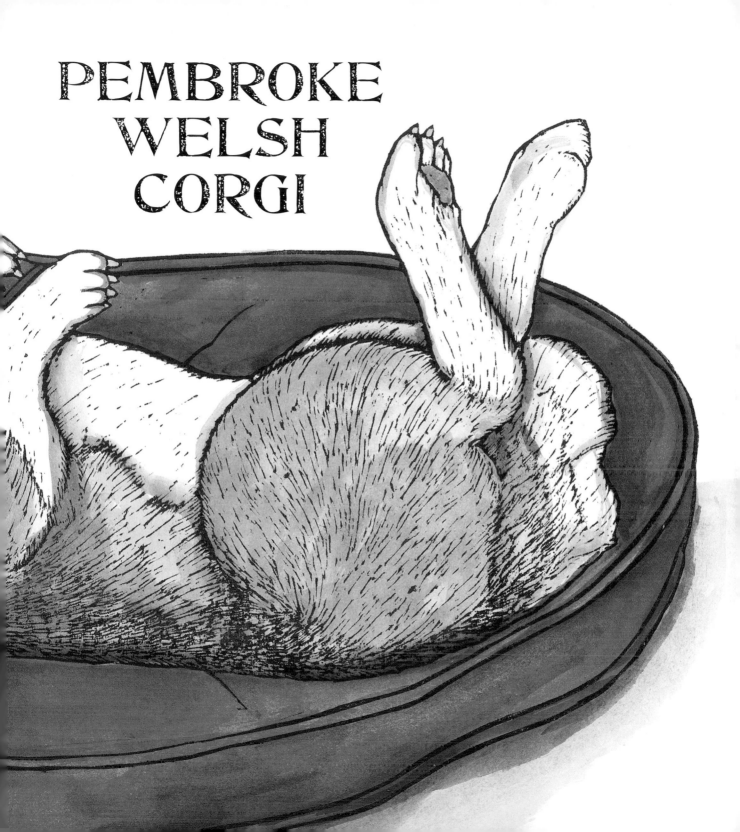

summer metronome
tongue darts in, out, as you do
doors revolve round you

staccato sniffing
fills your ribs' parentheses
you keep scent's secret

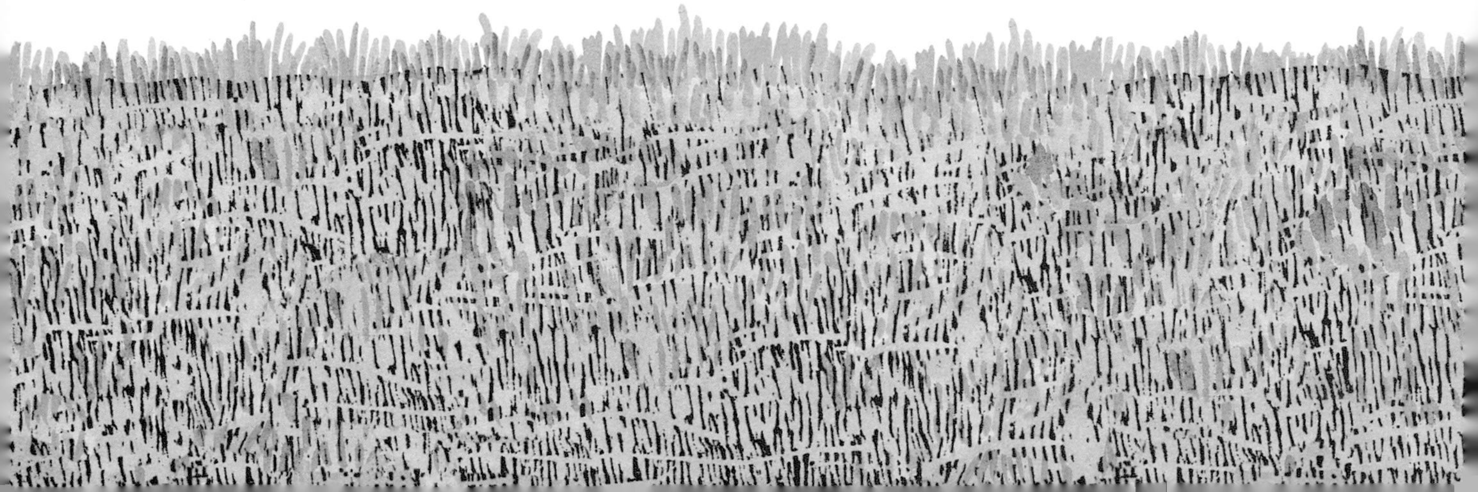

BLOODHOUND

GOLDEN RETRIEVER

stick like a wide grin
panting, chest-deep, in the lake
eye of each ripple

PARSON RUSSELL TERRIER

elbow-deep in dirt
nothing to bury but hours
holes are the treasure

wagging bobtailed dog
anything you touch joins in
joy is no phantom

ENGLISH SPRINGER
SPANIEL

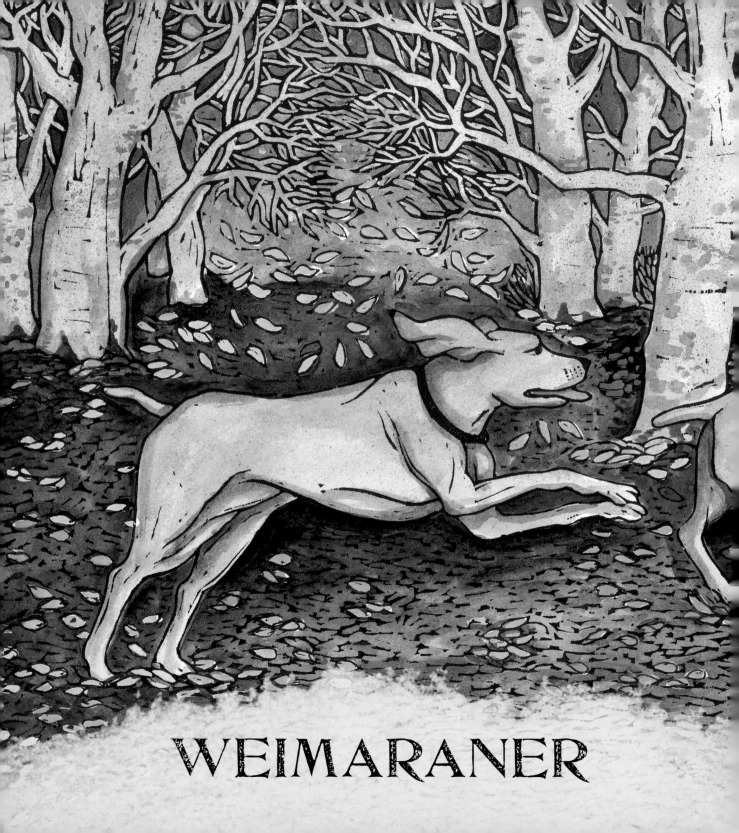

WEIMARANER

first frost, windless cold
dogs flush six deer in the woods
gold showers the chase

SAMOYED

giant pink curled snail:
tongue races across black lips
nothing beats that smile

SHIH TZU

toy dog's own toy chest:
snowman, hedgehog, fake steak, jet—
squeak is all they speak

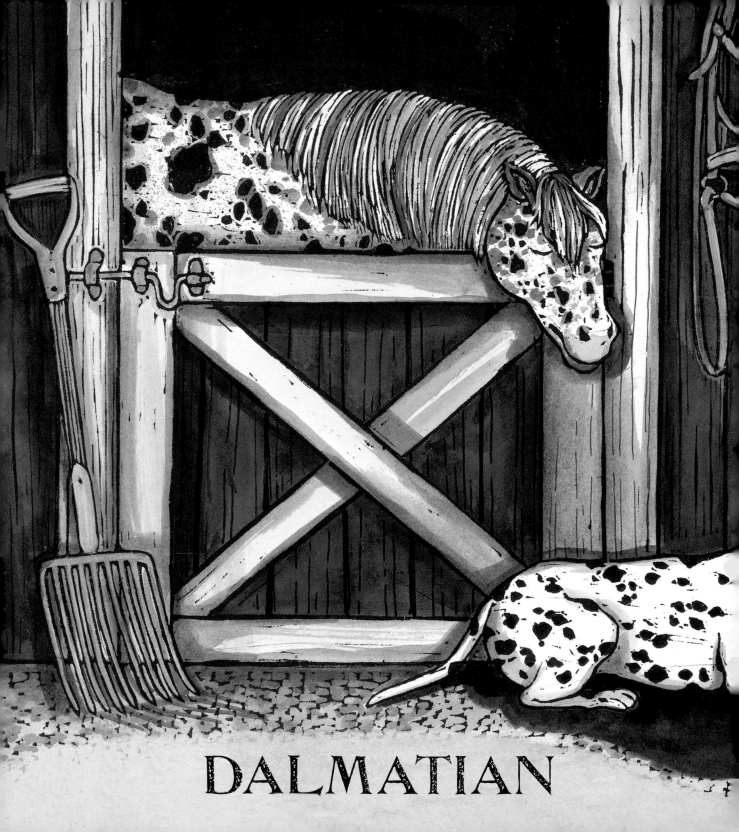

DALMATIAN

stable dogs sleeping
beside the Appaloosa
their shadows spotless

the one hieroglyph
that appears on all windows:
your nose writing *When?*

MINIATURE
SCHNAUZER

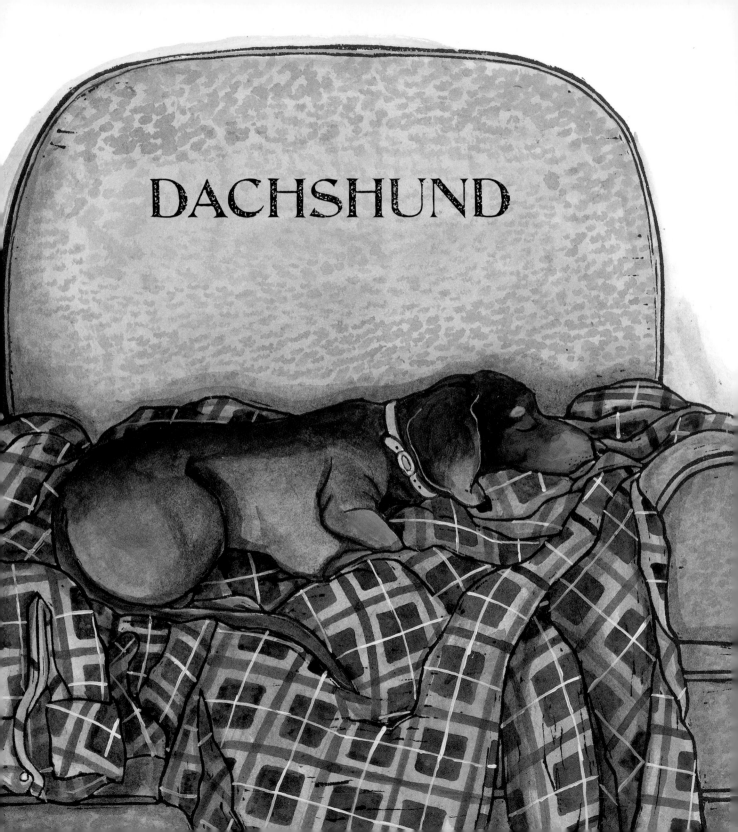

DACHSHUND

napping on a robe
that human's scent is your clothes
you will never change

Notes for Dog Lovers and Fans of Haiku

BLUETICK COONHOUND

 In rural Ohio, where I live, coonhounds — traditional hunting dogs — are popular companions. Hearty animals with short coats that don't tangle with seeds or burrs, they often bed down in straw-filled doghouses, toasty and content.

Dogs often circle before plopping down in a tight ball to sleep. That's a behavior inherited from their wild ancestors, who needed to mat down tall field grasses to create a comfortable den.

BORDER COLLIE

 Border collies live to work: moving herds of cattle from barn to pasture, protecting and tracking each cow and calf. In this poem, the cows are the stars that the border collie gazes at through the powerful "telescope" of its instincts. And the fact that cows give milk makes "Milky Way" a bit of a pun.

SIBERIAN HUSKY

 Huskies can be any number of thick-coated, sled-pulling dogs, but a Siberian husky is a specific arctic breed. These dogs are suited for cold, with a thick double-coat and "snowshoe" feet as well as extra hairs between the toes.

GREAT PYRENEES

 The Great Pyrenees, bred to guard sheep in the mountains that form the border between France and Spain, is a magnificent animal; its voluminous coat is as white as snow with pale beige markings, and its tail is long enough to touch the ground. When the Great Pyrenees gets excited, this tail waves a question mark high above the dog's body.

LABRADOR RETRIEVER

 My Lab Madison, like many web-footed retrievers, could not resist the chance to pursue waterfowl. Although he never outswam a duck or goose, he was not discouraged from splashing in for a chase.

The Labrador retriever, originally from Newfoundland, not Labrador (both are located along Canada's Atlantic coast), has been *the* most popular dog in America since 1991.

BEAGLE

There are two types of hounds: scent hounds, like the beagle, which use their noses to track prey; and sight hounds, or gazehounds, which use their keen eyesight. Beagles sometimes howl when other dogs bark, creating a canine chorus. In this poem, I imagine the voices of neighborhood dogs baying, howling, crooning, and mingling together like chimney smoke.

OLD ENGLISH SHEEPDOG

The Old English sheepdog is nicknamed the "bobtail" for its short or absent wagger. It sports a double coat of long, coarse outer hairs, with a dense, waterproof pile below that's nearly as thick as the coats of the sheep it guards. Keeping warm is no problem for a sheepdog! But staying cool? A sheepdog loves to chill down in a pond.

STANDARD POODLE

"Puppy breath," which, like a human baby's breath, smells of its mother's milk, is one of the sweetest and most fleeting things about a puppy. But at two or three months of age, just as their growing teeth and claws begin to make nursing uncomfortable for the mother, puppies begin eating solid food. Soon their tiny milk teeth are replaced by permanent teeth, and their soft, needle-sharp nails harden.

From 1960 through 1982, the poodle reigned as the most popular dog in America. Only the cocker spaniel's two reigns, decades apart and totaling twenty-five years, best the poodle's popularity.

PEMBROKE WELSH CORGI

Alert, stocky, and short, the corgi typically sleeps on its back with all four feet in the air or with its legs splayed out. By exposing its more vulnerable belly, the dog is showing that it's relaxed and happy in the pack. The name *corgi* comes from two Welsh words: *cor,* meaning "dwarf," and *qi,* meaning "dog." There are two breeds of corgis: the Pembroke Welsh corgi, which has a very short tail, and the longer-bodied Cardigan Welsh corgi, which has a long tail.

PUG

The pug is one of several breeds whose faces are "clenched," with a short muzzle and a face that's flattened. Its compact breathing structure causes pugs to grunt, snort, grumble, sneeze, snore, and pant. It can also make breathing difficult, especially in hot weather, when the pug's curled tongue pulses in and out with each pant.

BLOODHOUND

Humorously described as a "nose with a dog attached," the bloodhound is *the* legendary tracking dog, and the "noble blood" of its carefully bred ancestors gives the breed its name. The bloodhound's wrinkled brow and long, soft ears cup those scent molecules toward the 230 million olfactory receptors that line its nose. Humans have fewer than six million receptors.

GOLDEN RETRIEVER

I've owned four retrievers, and one was part water buffalo. At least, he *acted* like one, up to his armpits in a shallow pond, calmly watching the folks on shore. When he panted, the whole pond echoed his breathing, ripple after ripple.

PARSON RUSSELL TERRIER

Most dogs enjoy a little digging, but terriers—their very name comes from the Latin word for "ground," *terra*—were bred to chase varmints and to follow them, barking and burrowing, above- and underground. But dogs dig for other reasons as well: to remedy boredom, to escape confinement, to unearth something stinky (and possibly delicious!), or simply to create a cooler place to snooze on a hot day.

ENGLISH SPRINGER SPANIEL

Tails help dogs tell humans and other dogs what they're thinking: *I'm warning you! I'm so glad to see you! Let's play! I'm not so sure about you. . . .* So what if a dog has a short tail? More than fifty breeds either are born tailless or have their tails shortened at birth to prevent future injury or health problems. But you can still read the excitement in a dog like the English springer spaniel; its entire hindquarters wag and wiggle!

WEIMARANER

Nicknamed the "gray ghost," the Weimaraner possesses a sleek coat, blue-gray or amber eyes, a muscular build, and webbed feet for swimming. Thanks to William Wegman, the breed has reached superstar status in recent years.

SAMOYED

Can a dog smile? Panting can *look* like smiling, but that's just how dogs cool off. (They also sweat through their paws' pads.) What looks to humans like a happy grin — the corners of the mouth pulling back and up — means *You're the boss!* among dogs. It's how dogs settle things peacefully: a dominant animal growls, and a submissive animal grins. Samoyeds, with their outgoing personalities, are great smilers. Their fluffy, bright-white coat really sets off that large black grin.

SHIH TZU

Unless your dog has his or her own allowance, *you're* probably the one who picks out the squeaking cheeseburger or the fluffy woodchuck with the microchip that makes the chattering *chuck-chuck* sound, and your dog is the one who fetches it, gnaws it, or buries it among the bushes. But does he or she ever recognize those chewable items as cheeseburgers or woodchucks? No, the dog cares about the object's texture, smell, and sound. The shih tzu was bred to resemble a lion, a sacred beast revered by Chinese emperors. Pronounced "shee dzoo," its name means "lion" in Chinese.

DALMATIAN

Not many families with young children can provide enough work, training, and space for a dog originally bred to run alongside horse-drawn coaches. Yet, in 1966 (five years after the release of the movie *101 Dalmations*), this energetic, intelligent stable dog became the fifteenth most popular breed in the United States.

MINIATURE SCHNAUZER

Named for the German word for "muzzle," *schnauze,* this dog is beloved for its facial goatee, long "eyebrows," and happy-yappy attitude.

Dogs can't tell time as we do, but comfort and security for dogs comes from routines. They like knowing what's next: *If I sit, will there be a treat? Once you dress, we'll walk, right?* Their nose prints on car windows, picture windows, and doors are all signs in their "waiting rooms."

DACHSHUND

The dachshund, whose name combines the German words for "badger," *dachs,* and "dog," *hund,* is a hound descended from pointers and terriers. Trained to burrow into badger holes, these dogs are diggers, even if there's no badger within miles! But they are also devoted companion animals who love nothing more than snuggling with members of their pack. Dogs know us by our scents; for them, we are the smell of home.